THE M

by

Deanna (Marchionda) Rossi

in collaboration with
Jeff Levitan

The Gift of Money
Copyright © 2021 by Priorities Incorporated, LLC

All rights reserved. No part of this book may be reproduced or transmitted in any form or by any means without written permission from the author.

ISBN-9798707182815

Illustrated by Pamela Sobinovsky

Printed in USA

DEDICATION

This book is dedicated to my children…my true Gifts. Mya Colella you are the JOY of my life. Vito Colella you are the LOVE of my life. I wanted you both more than I can ever explain. All that I do, I do for the two of you.

SPECIAL THANKS

I now know why there are not simple books written on money! Thanks to my wonderful legal and compliance team that took on the daunting task to help me revise this book to make it compliant with all the rules and regulations in our industry. Unfortunately sometimes to comply with all the rules and regulations, some topics and descriptions became a little more verbose and intricate than I think the non-money person would find easy to read; however, we wanted to be sure we delivered to you something that was easy to understand yet accurate. I hope you appreciate these great minds as much as I do and always feel free to reach out for further clarification on any of these GIFTS of Money.

Table of Contents

Disclaimer 4
Foreword 6
Preface 7
Introduction 10
GIFT 1 : Rule of 72 14
GIFT 2 : Diversification 20
GIFT 3 : Taxes 22
GIFT 4 : Life Insurance 26
GIFT 5 : Dollar Cost Averaging 60
GIFT 6 : Tax Exemptions.........................66
GIFT 7 : Cost of Waiting..........................69
GIFT 8 : Debt Management.....................73
GIFT 9 : Mortgages 83
GIFT 10 : Planning 96

Disclaimer

The purpose of this book is to provide a general understanding about financial concepts and information. It is not intended to give advice on tax, insurance, investment, or any product or service. Since each of us has our own unique situation, you should have all the appropriate information to understand and make the right decision to fit with your needs and your financial goals. We hope that you will succeed in building your financial future.

Neither the author nor any other person associated with this book may be held liable for any damages that may result from the contents of this book.

No book can be a substitute for professional, personalized advice. Readers are encouraged to seek financial advice from qualified professionals, including licensed investment advisors, stockbrokers, accountants, insurance agents, attorneys, CPAs, and other qualified individuals.

Individual circumstances are a key factor in determining a course of action. The strategies in the book may not be appropriate for everyone. Consult a professional to help identify strategies that are appropriate for the particular situation.

Disclosure

Transamerica Financial Advisors, Inc. (TFA), Member FINRA, SIPC and Registered Investment Advisor, offers securities and Investment Advisory Services. World Financial Group Insurance Agency, LLC, World Financial Group Insurance Agency of Hawaii, Inc., World Financial Group Insurance Agency of Massachusetts, Inc., World Financial Insurance Agency, LLC and /or WFG Insurance Agency of Puerto Rico, Inc. (collectively WFGIA), offer insurance products. WFGIA and TFA are affiliated companies. WFGIA Headquarters: 11315 Johns Creek Parkway, Johns Creek, GA 30097-1517. Phone: 770.453.9300 TFA Headquarters: 570 Carillon Parkway, St. Petersburg, FL 33716. Phone: 770.248.3271 The views and opinions expressed thereon are those of the author, and not necessarily those of Transamerica Financial Advisors, Inc. or its affiliated companies Neither Transamerica Financial Advisors, Inc. (World Financial Group Insurance Agency, LLC) nor its representatives (agents) may provide tax or legal advice. Anyone to whom this material is promoted, marketed, or recommended should consult with and rely on their own independent tax and legal professionals regarding their particular situation and the concepts presented herein.

Foreword

Money is a GIFT. I don't mean that you haven't worked hard for it or that you don't deserve it. I mean that it is something to be cherished and utilized. Many people don't utilize money. They earn it but never utilize it correctly. Imagine if someone gave you a wonderful GIFT, a piece of jewelry let's say, and you never wore it. If you just put the GIFT somewhere for "safe keeping," the person that gave you the GIFT would be offended, wouldn't they? Especially if that jewelry was a certain ring... Even in a relationship, you may deserve the ring, the token of someone's affection and promise, but you had to work for it, and ultimately it is a GIFT. So is money. It is something to be cherished and utilized. It is something that represents what you have worked for and it is the ultimate GIFT if utilized correctly.

Preface

In the bible the parable of the talents illustrates the point that money *is* a GIFT:

THE PARABLE OF THE TALENTS

"For it will be like a man going on a journey, who called his servants and entrusted to them his property. To one he gave five talents, to another two, to another one, to each according to his ability. Then he went away. He who had received the five talents went at once and traded with them, and he made five talents more. So also he who had the two talents made two talents more. But he who had received the one talent went and dug in the ground and hid his master's money. Now after a long time the master of those servants came and settled accounts with them. And he who had received the five talents came forward, bringing five talents more, saying, 'Master, you delivered to me five talents; here I have made five talents more.' His master said to him, 'Well done, good and faithful servant. You have been faithful over a little; I will set you over much. Enter into the joy of your master.' And he also who had the two talents came forward, saying, 'Master, you delivered to me two talents; here I have made two talents more.' His master said to him, 'Well done, good and faithful servant. You have been faithful over a little; I will set you over much. Enter into the joy of your master.' He also who had received the one talent came forward, saying, 'Master, I knew you to be a hard man, reaping where you did not sow, and gathering where you scattered no seed, so I was afraid, and I went and hid your talent in the ground. Here you have what is yours.' But his master answered him, 'You wicked and slothful servant! You knew that I reap where I have not sown and gather where I scattered no seed? Then you ought to have invested my money with the bankers, and at my coming I should have received what was my own with interest. So, take the talent from him and give it to him who has the ten talents. For to everyone who has will more be given, and he will have an abundance. But from the one who has not, even what he has will be taken away. And cast the worthless servant into the outer darkness. In that place there will be weeping and gnashing of teeth."

-Matthew 25:14-30 English Standard Version (ESV)-

So, with that being said, surely the servant that buried the talent for "safe keeping" did not utilize the GIFT he was given, nor did he honor the GIFT. He offended the master. You offend yourself and your descendants every time you have even a penny and you waste it. I'm not saying not to spend your money, but I am saying that as with any GIFT, we have to cherish it and use it appropriately. For many people they would do as the third servant did. They would not know what to do with the money, so they would do nothing at all. It is said that **to make no choice at all is in fact a choice.**

Introduction

So, how do you utilize the GIFT of money? What should you do every time you earn, receive, or are blessed with the GIFT of money? How are we to be sure that we cherish that GIFT and let that GIFT bless others exponentially? Well, we must first learn the basics and then we must execute the concepts that we learn.

By 4th grade, children have learned how to divide; yet most often we don't teach them the practical application of division. Sure, we teach them that if you have a pie and you give half to your sister, how much do you have left? Half of a pie and childhood diabetes. But seriously, the point of education is that we are teaching our youth how to go get a job and make money. The problem is that we never teach our youth nor our adults in this country what *to do* with that money. So, the question becomes, how can you practically use that basic division as a GIFT? How about keeping you out of debt? How about making your money work hard for you so you don't have to work so hard for your money?

Sounds great, right?

Well, in this book you will find SIMPLE explanations of some of the basic financial concepts that the rich have been using for years, but the everyday person was never taught.

I was blessed to be in the right place at the right time at 22 years old. I had a business degree and had heard of many of these concepts, yet although I was able to match up the definition with the term on a multiple choice test in some basic finance or economics class in college, I really didn't know how to *use* these concepts. Luckily, I was taught these concepts and how to apply them. When I learned these concepts at age 22, I felt the world needed to learn them too. So I dove into a career in the financial industry. I knew that the world was dying financially and that I had the ability to help at my fingertips. I knew that alone I could not get the word out to enough people, so not only did I get licensed to become a financial advisor, I built a company of financial professionals that could help me spread the word of these simple, yet effective concepts. We still have yet to scratch the surface. So, I implore you to share these concepts as a GIFT to others, GIFT this book, and give the GIFT of your newfound knowledge with everyone you can! Give others the Gift of Money!

Maybe it is because I started in the industry at such a young age that I realized that the best way to share these concepts was not in "financialeese", but in simple language that even the inexperienced person could grasp. Or it could be that since I am a first generation American, I grew up around family members that didn't understand English very well and I was well versed in using small words and basic ideas to get big ideas across. In this book, you will find the charts and drawings that gave me the "AhhHaa moments". These are the charts and explanations that actually made me finally **understand** a concept I had once learned from a professor, that sometimes took an entire semester to explain in mathematical equations. Today I use this same information to educate clients. So yes, I can go into the algorithms and technical jargon and various explanations for each concept to prove the concept over and over. However, you will not find that in this book! This book breaks down the essentials into simple and easy to follow basics. You will find some explanations that may seem a bit verbose and that is to be sure all the information provided is fair and complete. As well as, you will see stated often that every situation is unique; which is true. So be sure to take that into consideration. These are the tools that every person needs to know about money. Use it as a reference guide.

Most importantly, don't just read through these concepts, be sure to *utilize* the concepts! Just as the 4th grader that learned division would fail his or her test if they don't apply what they learned, we as adults must apply what we learn to be successful. A GIFT is not a GIFT unless it is utilized. Use these GIFTs of Money.

GIFT ONE
THE RULE OF 72

The Rule of 72 is a mathematical concept that shows how long it will take for money to double. It illustrates the concept of compounding interest and it said that Albert Einstein called compounding interest the 8th wonder of the world, man's greatest invention!* I like to say that it shows you how to make money work harder for you so you don't have to work so hard for you money.

The way the Rule of 72 works is simple, yet extremely powerful. Take the number 72 and divide it by the interest rate. The answer to that division problem is roughly how many years it will take for money to nearly double.

$$\frac{72}{\text{Interest rate}} = \text{Years for money to nearly double}$$

*https://quotesonfinance.com/quote/79/albert-einstein-compound-interest

Let's be clear: It is important to understand that the Rule of 72 is merely a mathematical concept that can be used to help demonstrate how compounding interest works. Understand that most investments generate fluctuating returns, so the period in which an investment can double cannot be determined with certainty. The hypothetical examples provided below do not reflect any taxes, expenses, or fees associated with any specific investment. If these costs were reflected the amounts shown would be lower and the time to double would be longer. Investing involves risk including the potential loss of principal.

This is how I have seen the Rule of 72 illustrated with accuracy:*

72 ÷ 2% = 36 At 2% money nearly doubles every 36 years	
Years	Amount
Initial Amount	$10,000
35	$19,999
70	$39,996

72 ÷ 4% = 18 At 4% money nearly doubles every 18 years	
Years	Amount
Initial Amount	$10,000
18	$20,258
36	$41,039
53	$79,941

72 ÷ 6% = 12 At 6% money nearly doubles every 12 years	
Years	Amount
Initial Amount	$10,000
12	$20,122
24	$40,289
36	$81,473
48	$163,939

* *Rule of 72*
Divide 72 by an annual interest rate to calculate approximately how many years it takes for money to double (assuming the interest is compounded annually). Keep in mind that this is just a mathematical concept. Interest rates will fluctuate over time, so the period in which money can double cannot be determined with certainty. Additionally, this hypothetical example does not reflect any taxes, expenses, or fees associated with any specific product. If these costs were reflected the amounts shown would be lower and the time to double would be longer.

I have found that this chart is the easiest way to grasp the GENERAL CONCEPT of the rule *of 72 and compounding interest.*

Age	4%	Age	6%	Age	8%	Age	10%
Money nearly doubles 18 years		Money nearly doubles 12 years		Money nearly doubles 9 years		Money nearly doubles 7.2 years	
29	$10,000	29	$10,000	29	$10,000	29	$10,000
47	$20,000	41	$20,000	38	$20,000	36	$20,000
65	$40,000	53	$40,000	47	$40,000	43	$40,000
		65	$80,000	56	$80,000	50	$80,000
				65	$160,000	57	$160,000
						65	$320,000
						72	$640,000

This chart has been rounded to the nearest $1,000 and number of years it takes to nearly double money. It is THE chart of the Rule of 72 that really allowed me to understand the concept.

All figures are for illustrative purposes only and do not reflect an actual investment in any product. They do not reflect the performance risks, expenses or charges associated with any actual investment. Past performance is not an indication of future performances. The Rule of 72 is a mathematical concept that approximates the number of years it would take to nearly double the principal at a constant rate of return. The performance of investments fluctuates over time, and as a result, the actual time it will take an investment to nearly double in value cannot be predicted with any certainty. Additionally, there are no guarantees that any investment or savings program can outpace inflation. Please note that high risk has been historically associated with high returns.

As you can see in the illustration, if 72 is divided by a 4% annual rate of return it would take roughly 18 years for money to nearly double. At a 6% rate of return, money would nearly double in nearly 12 years. So, just a 2% difference annually can have a meaningful impact over time.

Now, what if the annual interest rate were doubled? What affect do you think this would have on money over time? Most people say they think it would double. But this concept illustrates COMPOUNDING interest and the result will actually increase exponentially! 72 divided by 8 is 9; so if an 8% annual rate of return were applied, money would nearly double every 9 years.

That means that given two scenarios, both with a beginning balance of $10,000 and obtaining an 8% annual rate of return versus a 4% annual rate of return, money would not just simply nearly double, rather it nearly *quadruples*! This is due to compounding interest over time.

So, would you agree that you need to be fighting for every single percentage point increase in annual rate of return that you can get?

Well, if you are only investing in a mere savings account and are getting a tiny rate of return, it may be time to look elsewhere to invest. But, does that mean you should put all your of your money in one investment?

GIFT TWO
DIVERSIFICATION

The answer is NO. No one should put all of their money in one investment as it is important to be diversified. Remember the old saying, "don't put all your eggs in one basket"? Well, that is *diversification*.

This chart illustrates it well.

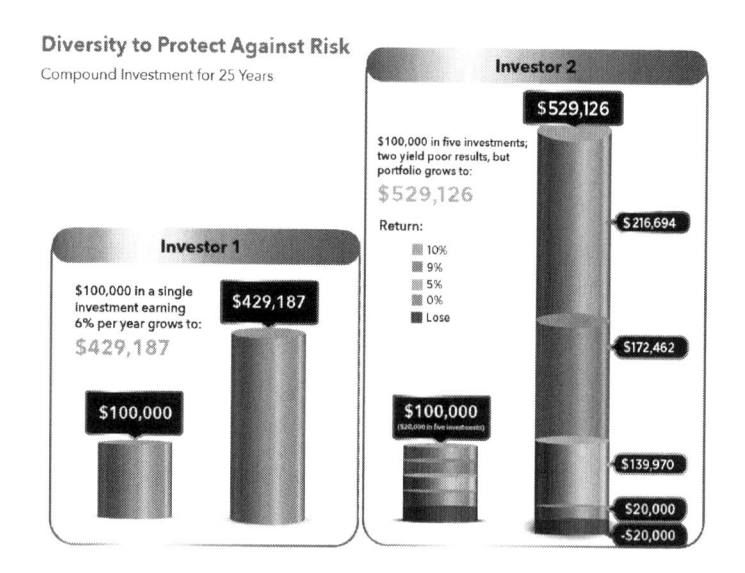

Diversity to Protect Against Risk
Compound Investment for 25 Years

Investor 1
$100,000 in a single investment earning 6% per year grows to:
$429,187

Investor 2
$100,000 in five investments; two yield poor results, but portfolio grows to:
$529,126

Return:
- 10% $216,694
- 9% $172,462
- 5% $139,970
- 0% $20,000
- Lose -$20,000

$100,000 (\$20,000 in five investments)

The hypothetical rates of return shown are assumed on a $100,000 investment compounded for 25 years. These figures are for illustrative purposes only and do not represent the past or the future performance of any actual investments. There is no assurance that a diversified investment portfolio will achieve a better return than a non-diversified one. These figures do not reflect any fees or charges associated with any investment. If they did, they would be lower than cited above.

This shows an investor in a single investment getting a 6% annual rate of return. Starting with an investment of $100,000, their money would grow to $429,187 after 25 years. Yet, someone who is diversified and even loses money on one portion of their investment, makes 0%, 8%, 9%, and 10% on the other portions, would out earn the person with the 6% flat rate of return! Actually, the concepts around diversification won a Nobel Prize in 1990. The bible even references this in Ecclesiastes 11:2 *Apportion what you have into seven, or even eight parts, because you don't know what disaster might befall the land.*

That being said, would you like to be **diversified**?

Diversification can help in many scenarios; however, risk and, in particular, systematic risk cannot be eliminated. Even properly diversified portfolios can and do lose money.

GIFT THREE
TAXES

So, now let's assume you are getting a positive rate of return and you are properly diversified. The only problem would be that you would actually be **making** money, and when you make money in this country you have a partner. Who is that partner? Uncle Sam. Now Uncle Sam is going to take a portion of your money whether you like it or not. The thing is, he doesn't think he is so bad because he gives you *choices* as to how you can pay him *his* portion. I always look at it as if he gives you from 3 buckets to choose. As you can see from the shaded portion of this graphic, different investment choices can provide various opportunities to be taxed.

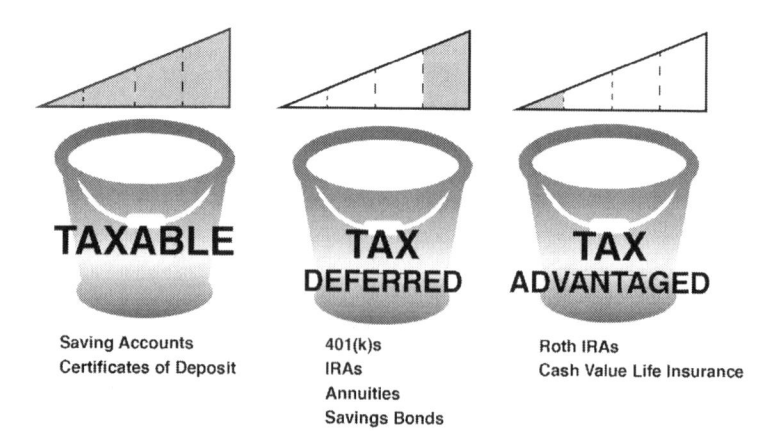

TAXABLE
Saving Accounts
Certificates of Deposit

TAX DEFERRED
401(k)s
IRAs
Annuities
Savings Bonds

TAX ADVANTAGED
Roth IRAs
Cash Value Life Insurance

The **Taxable** bucket includes Savings Accounts and Certificates of Deposit (CDs), and the like. These accounts are taxable on the front end, when you earn the money, then you pay capital gains taxes when you earn interest or dividends in these accounts as well.

The **Tax-Deferred** bucket includes 401(k), other Employer Sponsored Plans, IRAs (Individual Retirement Accounts), Annuities and Saving Bonds and they are taxable on the back end. So, there are no taxes up front when the money is earned, but you pay taxes when you take the money out.

The **Tax-Advantaged** bucket includes Roth IRAs and Cash Value Life Insurance products, which are taxed on the front end.*

So, between Taxable, Tax-deferred, and Tax-advantaged, in which bucket would you rather have your money?

---

* The main purpose of a cash value life insurance policy is to provide a death benefit. It is not a short-term savings vehicle nor is it ideal for short-term insurance needs. It is designed to be long term in nature and should be purchased only if you have the financial ability to keep it in-force for a substantial period of time.

The Gift of Tax-Advantaged Accounts
Roth IRA

A Roth IRA is an account that if you take the money out prior to 59 ½ you will be subject to ordinary income taxes and a 10% withdrawal penalty on any gain in the account, unless it is a qualified distribution.* Besides that, you can access the money you put in (also known as your initial contribution) tax-free. However, there is a limit as to how much you can contribute and it's currently about $6,000 per year. Many people need to put away a lot more to reach their retirement goals than $6,000 per year. If you are older than 50 you can contribute a maximum of $7,000 per year. So, this is very limiting for a lot of people. Also, there is an income limit, if you make too much money, you are not allowed to contribute to a Roth IRA.

*A qualified distribution from a Roth IRA only happens if you have had the money in for 5 years. At that point only upon death, disability, or for a first-time home purchase can you pull the money out without incurring the penalty.

The Gift of Tax-Advantaged Accounts
Other Tax Advantaged Vehicles

Besides investment and savings vehicles, there are actually some Health Insurance and Life Insurance Products that are also considered Tax-Advantaged.

The gains in Cash Value Life Insurance Products are also categorized in the Tax Advantaged Bucket. Cash Value Life Insurance itself is not categorized as an investment nor savings vehicle and is **not a retirement plan**; therefore, with Cash Value Life Insurance, there is no age 59 ½ requirement, so there is no 10% penalty. *

When people hear these benefits they want to know more; so, I'll explain Cash Value Life Insurance in more detail in the next chapter.

Note: If a policy lapses with an outstanding loan, or if gains in the policy are withdrawn before age 59 1/2, there could be tax consequences and a 10% penalty.

GIFT Four
Life Insurance

There are two general types of Life Insurance.

Term and **Permanent**.

Term is like renting a house. You have a certain "term" in which you are insured. You pay a fixed amount each month and at the end of the term your policy expires. Like renting, at the end of the rental agreement your cost could go up. You see, if you out-live the term and would like to get another term policy, the cost of doing so will likely be higher due to your increased age and potential health issues later in life. Many policies offer an option to renew, but again at much higher rates.

Term insurance serves a purpose for many people. It is relatively inexpensive compared to a permanent life insurance policy. It is a great way to be sure to help protect a family from financial burdens in the event of an untimely death. However, term insurance is not right for everyone. The cost of any type of life insurance varies depending on sever factors including age, gender, overall health, and the amount of coverage. Consider the particular situation and consult the appropriate professional.

Term Insurance can be especially useful in temporary situations. Think of the med-school student with a family. The student would tend to be young and healthy, have a sizeable student loan, expenses of a family, and will have a significantly larger income in the future once the MD follows the name. This individual may choose the cheaper Term Policy during med-school so that it is affordable in the short term just to cover the family in case of the unspeakable. Then, once the student becomes a doctor and makes more money, assuming they maintained their health and good rating, they would likely try to get **Permanent** policy.

Permanent is the other type of insurance and is also called cash value insurance. Permanent insurance can be compared to buying a house because as you pay for a house, it builds equity. Permanent insurance builds cash value. In some cases you can eventually pay off a house. Likewise, Permanent insurance can eventually have enough cash value to allow the owner to stop making payments and fund the expenses within the policy. With a house, you can borrow from the equity, and you have a permanent "roof over your head" if you choose to fund it properly. The same goes for Permanent insurance. There is an ability to access some of the policy value and if you choose to fund it properly it can last until death.

Like owning a home, permanent insurance is not right for everyone. Consider the particular situation and consult the appropriate professional when deciding if Permanent Life Insurance is appropriate.

To keep it simple there are 4 types of policies in this permanent category:

Whole Life

Universal Life

Indexed Universal Life

Variable Universal Life

Whole Life and **Universal Life** work similarly. Both types provide a guaranteed interest rate set by the insurance company. Whole Life insurance has a fixed premium amount while Universal Life insurance gives a policyholder more flexibility in the premium payments and death benefit.

Think of Whole Life and Universal Life insurances as having two elements. A life insurance death benefit (also known as the Face Amount) attached to a policy value that receives a guaranteed interest rate.

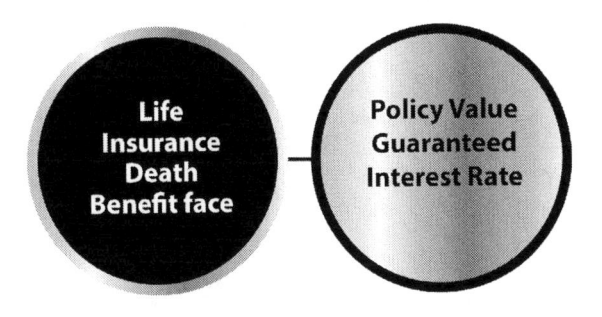

Life Insurance Death Benefit face — **Policy Value Guaranteed Interest Rate**

Let's be clear: Guarantees are based on the claims paying ability of the issuing insurance company. There are several fees and charges associated with permanent life insurance, including the cost of insurance charge, policy fees, various administrative charges, and rider charges. Permanent life insurance premiums are used to cover these charges, and then a portion goes towards the policy value. Whereas, Term insurance premium is only paying for the cost of insurance and expenses. This is why Permanent Insurance Premiums are higher than term.

And yet another reminder, the main purpose of life insurance is to provide a death benefit. Life insurance is not a short-term savings vehicle nor is it ideal for short-term insurance needs. It is designed to be long term in nature and should be purchased only if you have the financial ability to keep it in force for a substantial period of time.

Unlike term insurance, a Permanent Insurance policy will remain in force for as long as you continue to pay your premiums; hence, being considered Permanent Insurance. The issuing life insurance company guarantees a fixed interest rate on Whole Life and Universal Life Insurance policies. Over the years of serving families I have seen that for many companies the fixed interest rate ranges from 3-4%. *

*https://www.policygenius.com/life-insurance/whole-life-insurance-rates/

The other forms of permanent life insurance are **IUL** and **VUL**.

Think of these as life insurance policies that have the potential to accumulate cash value at a non-guaranteed interest rate. The Policy Value is also referred to as the Cash Value. Again the life insurance can last your entire life and to access any built up cash value you can take a withdrawal or borrow the money out as a loan. The best part of these two types of Permanent policies is their potential for increasing the policy's cash value.

Keep in mind that also means there is a potential for underperformance in VUL and volatility in interest crediting for IUL. It is possible that little or no interest could be credited for certain periods with IUL. Therefore, IUL and VUL policies are not right for everyone. Consider the particular situation and consult the appropriate professional when deciding if an IUL or a VUL is the right course of action.

Let's be Clear: As we discuss these forms of life insurance keep in mind that IUL has the potential for greater tax-deferred cash value accumulation when compared to a regular fixed universal life insurance product. However, since a portion of the credited interest is calculated by reference to an outside index, there is the potential for greater volatility in the interest amounts credited. VULs offer the unique feature of allowing the policy owner to invest their net premiums in a variety of investment options with a range of risk/reward potential. Although VULs offer growth potential of the policy's cash value, the investment options are subject to market risk and are subject to loss of principal.

The IUL

IUL stands for **Indexed Universal Life insurance** and the interest credited on the Policy Value is based in part on one or more financial market indices performance. (Although interest is based partly on outside index performance, IUL is not a security and index universal life insurance policies are not an investment in the stock market or in financial market indexes.) The rate of interest you could receive on the cash value can fluctuate from one time frame to another depending on the performance of the index that is being used to determine the rate of interest that you will receive during a certain segment of time in your particular policy. With most IUL policies there is a *guarantee element!* For example, some companies will *guarantee* a minimum interest rate, so that if the index goes down during a certain period you have some downside protection. Many IULs currently available also have a maximum rate or a cap that limits the rate of interest that can be credited to the policy.

Take note that the maximum rate usually has the ability to be changed by the insurance company at their discretion. Furthermore, if a policy is surrendered during the surrender period, significant charges can result in the policy owner receiving less than the total premiums paid into the policy.

For example if the index goes up 25%, your policy may have a maximum of 15%. The 15% would be the maximum rate used to calculate the interest credited to your policy. And this type of policy has a minimum guaranteed interest rate. Typically the minimum would be 0%.

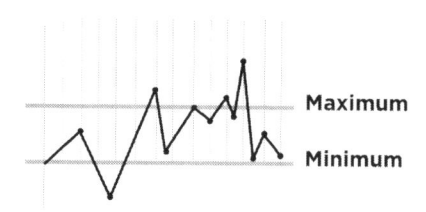

The IUL has a Life Insurance Death Benefit and a Policy Value. The Policy Value is the portion that is dependent on the performance of the index.

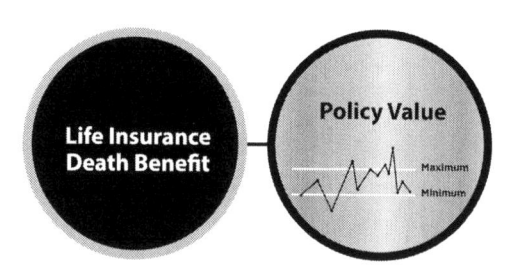

The VUL

VUL stands for Variable Universal Life insurance. **VUL is considered a security, like mutual funds or stocks, overseen by regulators and the US Securities and Exchange Commission.** Although they are issued by insurance companies, they are considered securities. This means that financial professionals must be appropriately licensed to sell this type of product.

It is called Variable because the cash value will vary with the market based on the investment selection that the client makes in the subaccounts. "Subaccount" is another name for the investment options available to the policy owner. Although the investments in the subaccounts may be well diversified, this type of investment does not come without risk. The Policy Value is dependent on the performance of the subaccounts and since subaccounts may include stocks, bonds, derivatives, commodities, money market instruments, or other investments, there is a potential for the subaccounts to perform negatively if the selected investments perform negatively. This means you can lose money and may lapse unless you pay additional premiums.

Subaccounts are not to be confused with a mutual fund. Although many subaccounts are often managed by mutual fund companies and in some cases are very similar to the company's mutual fund itself, they are not the same. They have different inception dates, daily prices and performance, costs, fees and capital gains distributions.

The VUL has a Life Insurance Death Benefit and a Policy Value. The Policy Value is the portion that is dependent on the performance of the subaccounts.

Life Insurance Death Benefit — **Policy Value**

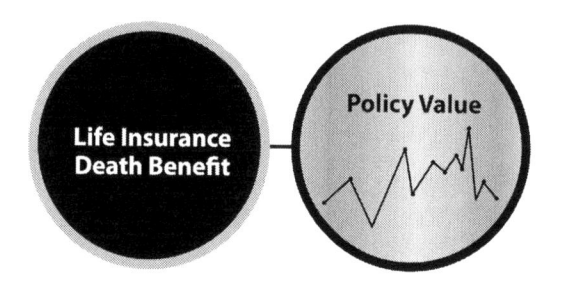

Since the subaccounts are investment options that are directly involved in the stock markets, a VUL has the possibility of loss of principal.* Your choice of investment options would depend on your particular risk tolerance. This is where a properly licensed individual should be consulted to determine if this may be an appropriate life insurance policy for some individuals.

* *Past performance is no guarantee of future performance. Both the return and principal value of subaccounts will fluctuate so that when redeemed, they may be worth more or less than their original cost. VULs are sold by prospectus that contains complete information about each VUL including fees, investment objectives, surrender charges, risks, expenses and other important information. Carefully consider all these important factors and read the prospectus carefully before investing. VUL investment options are subject to market risk and may lose value.*

Now that we understand some of the basics about the different types of life insurance, we need to have an important discussion about how these policies are structured, how they are taxed, and the costs associated with these policies. Furthermore, we must talk about the NEED for life insurance.

Only if someone has a need for Life Insurance should these vehicles even be considered. Although the IRS treats the gains favorably, there are costs and fees involved in a life insurance policy that would not be incurred with other types of accounts so the potential tax benefit may be outweighed by the cost. You see the primary purpose of life insurance is to provide a death benefit. There must be an insurable interest with a need for life insurance.

Cash value life insurance has the added benefit of the potential to build cash value over time. Once the cash value is sufficient, it may be withdrawn or loaned from the policy. Unless you are overfunding a policy, most of the premium paid may be going to cost of insurance and other policy related expenses and a small portion to cash value. Let me explain.

The different types of Cash Value Life Insurance discussed above are all **Life insurance** attached to a **Policy Value**. Yet, we saw above that depending on the type of policy, the Policy Value can grow in different ways.

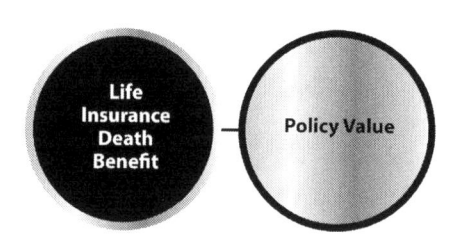

Life Insurance Death Benefit — Policy Value

So, let's say you have $250,000 of life insurance. When you pass away, your beneficiaries will get the life insurance generally federal income Tax Free. Now, I know you are thinking: "Ok well, I'm dead and they are running off with the money tax-free!? Can I access any of the money tax-free while I'm still living?" Yes, according to the Internal Revenue Code, the IRS says that you can *borrow* against the policy value Tax Free.

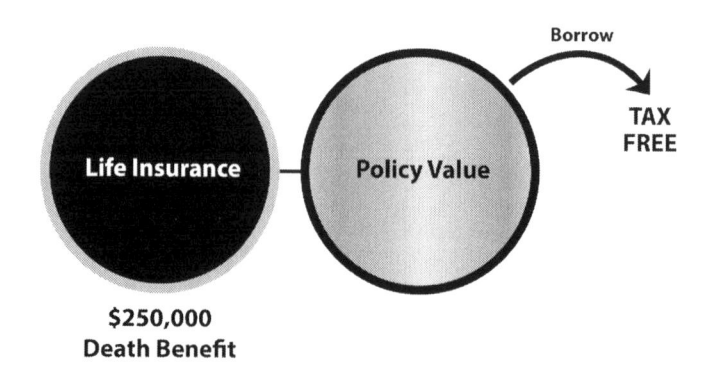

Life Insurance — Policy Value — Borrow TAX FREE

$250,000 Death Benefit

But, what is the key word there?

BORROW.

What happens when you borrow?

You have to pay it back.

With?

Interest!

You can borrow from the Policy Value tax-free while you are still living in the form of Tax Free loans. Policy loans are generally not taxable when taken and cash withdrawals are not taxable until they exceed the cost basis of the policy. So, if you take the money out as a loan you will get that money tax-free. But who wants to pay back interest? And who wants to be paying interest back during retirement?

Well, many companies have Cash Value Life Insurance. As we illustrated above, I have seen some companies charge up to 6-8%* interest especially in Whole Life and Universal Life insurance policies while other companies allow clients to borrow out at just 0-1%** interest. The lower rates are typically found in IUL and VUL products. But, loan rates vary by company and product. I have seen companies that offer VUL and IUL that have high loan rates too, so do your research and choose wisely. Reaching out to a properly licensed individual that can evaluate various companies and products is encouraged. Another thing to consider is you don't have to wait until age 59 ½, nor worry about a 10% penalty when utilizing these loans.

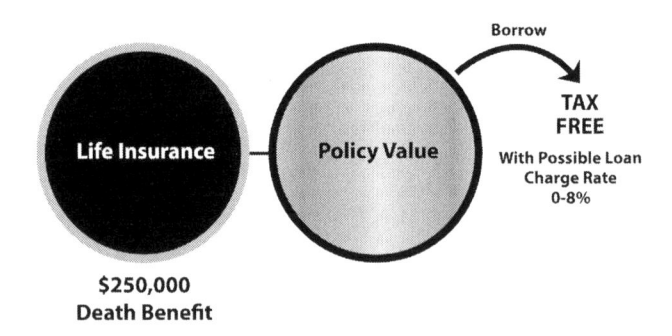

Life Insurance — **Policy Value** — Borrow → **TAX FREE** With Possible Loan Charge Rate 0-8%

$250,000 Death Benefit

*https://www.valuepenguin.com/life-insurance/borrow-against-life-insurance

**https://cdn.brandfolder.io/86JM1UOD/as/qf9nj0-bbhhuo-fv7sa7/FFIUL_Agent_Guide_Brochure.pdf

The Catch?: Loans will reduce the death benefit dollar for dollar, ongoing premiums must be met, and an increased amount of premium may be needed to keep the policy in-force and to avoid a lapse. Basically what that means is, if the Policy Value runs out, there can be many adverse effects like not having Life Insurance in force at the time of death, tax consequences like having to pay the 10% tax penalty or taxation as ordinary income on amounts received from loans and withdrawals, and the possibility to incur additional penalties depending on the policy owner's age, fees, or increased premiums. So, when considering a loan from a policy all of these consequences need to be considered.

The loans do usually have a credit. You see the insurance company will usually credit interest on the amount of the policy value that is allocated for a loan. What that means is, let's say you borrow in the first 10 years of the policy, you may be charged 2 ¾% interest and on your statement you will see loan interest charged. On the same statement the insurance company applies a credit to your account of 2%. That makes your *net* loan rate ¾%.

Since it is a "loan" the borrowed amount is Tax Free (as long as the policy is in force). The same concept applies after 10 years* on any loans from the policy value's gains with these companies, but if you take a loan at 2 ¾% they just credit your account back the entire 2 ¾%. This is known as a "wash loan" since in essence you pay 0% in interest.

*Each policy is different and the timeline for loan credits varies from policy to policy.

I get asked often, what about the money I contributed, can I get to that tax free? Yes you can withdrawal the money you put in and it is not subject to taxes. **Withdrawals** are tax-free up to the basis in the policy. Loans are tax-free as long as the policy stays in force.

Yet, taking loans and withdrawals could cause the policy's death benefit to be reduced. Premium payment most often must continue or even increase, otherwise the policy may lapse.

So, it sounds good, right? Most people think there has got to be another catch…well, there is. Since it is life insurance, not everyone qualifies for it or it may cost too much because the costs depend on the age, gender, health, and other risk factors of the proposed insured!

Let's talk about Costs.

Cost of Insurance

If you need life insurance and apply for a policy, in most cases, you will have to complete a medical evaluation. Basically you pay a deposit (called an initial premium) along with the application and the insurance company will send a professional out to the house to weigh you, measure you, take some blood and urine, and then they send the results to the insurance company. The company then determines the costs based on your health and risk factors. If you agree to costs in the terms of the contract, the initial premium will be credited to the policy. If you or the insurance company determine not to issue the policy, your premium will be returned to you.

The process to determine your cost of insurance is called *underwriting* and it usually takes 6 weeks to 2 months to get an answer. Have your agent give you brochures and links to materials to read over the details. You should review all the details and get a copy of all of the appropriate disclosures, details about charges, surrendering early, provisions, etc.

Premium Expense Charge

One of the terms I find that most people misunderstand is **Premium**. People tend to think the Premium is the total cost of the policy. That is sometimes true with term, but with Cash Value Life Insurance the Premium is merely the amount you pay into the policy. Many companies have a Premium Expense Charge on every dollar you contribute before anything else happens with your money.

The Premium Expense Charge is one of my pet peeves and is often overlooked by agents. It can be quite pricey and is usually a percentage of the premium. I have seen companies charge 10% on every dollar a client pays before any other fees are taken out. I have also seen policies with much lower rates. Premium and Expense charges should be considered carefully as it could allow someone to have more coverage at a much lower overall cost.

Fees

Besides Premium Expense charges, there could also be per unit charges, monthly policy charges, additional rider charges, fund fees on Variable products, monthly charges for the index account on Indexed products, and various other administrative fees. These are in addition to the Cost of The Insurance.

The Cost of the Insurance was discussed earlier. It is the cost that is determined during underwriting and is based on the age, gender, health, and other risk factors of the insured. Although one company may have a lower Cost of Insurance, the other fees should be considered to see if the policy is actually cost effective.

Some people ask me if Life Insurance is even worth it when there are so many fees. That's a personal question. How valuable is your life to your family or even to your business? There are many reasons for life insurance, but it is also a decision that must be made carefully. I view it like having children. There will be many costs associated with having a child and for many people they will have a child at any cost. They will jump through hoops to have a child and do just about anything to be sure they provide for their children. Some people view Life Insurance the same way. They will jump through all of the underwriting "hoops" to get the policy and they will do everything in their power to fund it. For others, having kids is not worth the cost or frustration, so they will avoid that responsibility at all costs. Similarly, some people don't see the value in Life Insurance.

Don't get me wrong, just because you don't have kids does not mean that you may not have a need for Life Insurance. Life Insurance serves many purposes from protecting families, protecting businesses, as well as even funding charities. There are also various tax benefits when it comes to life insurance. We mentioned earlier that the death benefit pays out to the beneficiary Tax Free.

Remember that all forms of permanent insurance also fall in the Tax-Advantaged category. What this means is you do not have to pay taxes on withdrawals up to the cost basis of the policy *nor* on the loans as they are Tax Free as long as you keep the policy active by paying enough premium. This makes permanent life insurance policies worth considering for people who have a need for life insurance and would like the potential for cash value accumulation.

Back in 1980's when the type of Cash Value Life Insurance known as Variable Universal Life Insurance (VUL) came to market, there was no limit on how much premium could be paid into these policies. So, many wealthy individuals started buying tiny life insurance policies and putting tons of cash into the Policy Value so they could earn interest and take money out tax-free. But, now there is a maximum as to how much you can put into a policy and still qualify for the tax benefits associated with Cash Value Life Insurance.

If this maximum, known as the 7 pay premium limit, is exceeded, the policy becomes a Modified Endowment Contract (MEC). This can result in some adverse tax consequences. Once a policy becomes a MEC, this classification cannot be reversed. The premium limit is based on various factors like the age of the insured, the face amount of the policy, and the ratio between premium paid and the face amount. To increase the 7 pay maximum, the face amount would have to be increased which usually requires the insured to go through underwriting again.

To sum this up and make it very clear, there are various fees and charges that apply with a cash value life insurance policy. Distributions such as loans and withdrawals can only be made if the policy has been in force long enough to accumulate sufficient value. Loans and withdrawals will reduce the policy value and death benefit. Loans are subject to interest charges. If a policy lapses while a loan is outstanding adverse tax consequences may result. Most companies also have surrender charges if a client cancels or withdraws cash from the policy in the first 5-20 years. Withdrawals can also be taken tax free up to the policy basis and when loans or withdrawals are taken the policy's total death benefit and cash surrender value will likely be reduced. Fees and charges also apply and the policy may lapse if too much is withdrawn or borrowed from the policy. Surrender charges apply if the policy lapses or a client surrenders the policy. Life insurance may not be suitable for everyone; therefore, it is important to consult a properly licensed professional.

Furthermore, it is important to understand that a VUL is a life insurance policy whose main purpose is to provide a death benefit. The policy is not a short-term savings vehicle nor is it ideal for short-term insurance needs. It is designed to be long-term in nature and should be purchased only if you have the financial ability to keep it in force for a substantial period of time. Net premiums invested into variable universal life subaccounts are subject to market risk. Policy values will increase or decrease depending on the investment experience of the underlying funds. When redeemed they may be worth less than the original cost. Contact a financial professional for a prospectus that contains complete information about VULs including fees, investment objectives, surrender charges, risks, expenses and other important information. Please carefully consider all these important factors and read the prospectus carefully before investing.

I'm also going to tell you my story, but before I do, do you see a theme here? Just because this was right for me does not make it right for everyone. The investment products and strategies I'm about to discuss may not be suitable for everyone. Each individual needs to consider their particular situation, and consult the appropriate professional. I'm glad I did!

Power of a Plan

Before I started in the industry, I had a ROTH IRA and a decreasing term policy. I thought I was on my game!! At 22 years old I had a retirement account and life insurance and I owned a home. The problem was, I had done some*thing*; but, not the "right *thing*s".

Two years earlier, I had a chunk of money to invest so I went to a rep that had just started at a local firm affiliated with one of the largest, Most Well-Known investment firms in the industry. I did not meet the company's minimum account size; but, since our families were friends and he was just getting started, he opened an account for me.

He never asked me any questions about my intentions for the money and just invested it in some stocks in a ROTH IRA. I was invested in Pepsi and I remember thinking: "I don't even like Pepsi, why wouldn't he invest in Coca-Cola? I don't want to support a company that I don't even buy their product." But, I figured he knew more than me.

I wish I had asked more questions. You see, not every product and strategy is right for everyone and my objectives did not fit into the ROTH IRA.

I also had bought a house; so, I went to my car insurance guy that worked for one of the largest, well-known insurance companies in the industry and asked him what I should do for life insurance. He put my husband and I in a decreasing term policy that would decrease over time to cover the mortgage on the house.

Again there is not a one-size-fits-all approach to life insurance and investments. I thought I had done the right thing by consulting professionals. Consulting professionals to educate you on what would be a suitable product or service for you may be the right course of action. The problem was that both of these "professionals" did not utilize one of the most essential elements of finance! They did not have a PLAN!

They did not know MY PLAN! Therefore, their products were not conducive to my long-range plan. Ask anyone who has ever met me. I now am somewhat obsessed with always asking people "What is your long range plan?" It probably all stemmed from this experience that shaped my life.

Luckily I was referred to a "true professional" that had various licenses and within an hour I was educated on the concepts in this book. This "true professional" was a financial advisor and did a FREE financial PLAN for me. He looked at where I wanted to go and looked at where I was currently financially and put together a road map for me to reach my financial paradise. The PLAN made me question the actions of my "so-called professionals." So, I went to the friend from the big investment firm.

I asked, "Why did you put me in a ROTH IRA?"

He said, "Because of the tax benefits."

I said, "Well, this other guy is telling me about a VUL. Why didn't you offer me a VUL?"

He said, "I'm not licensed to do so." He had an investment license (Series 7) but did not have a life insurance license.

I said, "Well does someone at your company have an insurance license?"

Well sure they did, but then he wouldn't have been my rep nor made the commission... and the properly licensed rep probably would not have done the account for me since I did not meet the company's minimum anyway. I told him to liquidate my account before I had any more gains. I took the 10% hit so I wouldn't suffer the 10% hit on an even larger amount later.

I then called my car insurance guy.

I asked him, "Why did you put me in a decreasing term policy?"

He said, "Because it was cheap and would cover the mortgage over 30 years."

I said, "Well this is just a tiny starter home and I never intended to stay here for 30 years, so why would I want a *decreasing* term policy when my need for insurance will *increase*?"

Since my husband and I needed the other's income to be able to afford not just the home, but the rest of our lifestyle, we were dramatically *under* insured.

I asked him. "Why didn't you offer me a VUL that is permanent?"

He said, "I'm not licensed to do so."

I asked, "Is there was anyone at your company that has both licenses?"

Of course there was, but then he couldn't be the agent and wouldn't have made the commission. I cancelled that decreasing term policy and bought a VUL. I was so passionate about sharing my new knowledge that I convinced the man that initially educated me to train me to do what he did. And the rest is history.

Just because this was right for me does not make it right for everyone. The point of the story is not all investment products and strategies may be suitable for all people. Mind you the permanent policy had more costs associated with it than the term and the VUL is not a retirement plan nor a loan vehicle. Individuals need to consider their particular situation, and consult the appropriate professional. Can you see now why I'm so glad I did?

Amount of Insurance

I mentioned in the story that I was **under-insured**. How much is enough and how much is too much?

One common rule of thumb people use to determine how much life insurance they need is to have **10 times their income** in life insurance.

If you make $50,000 per year your family will need a minimum of $500,000 in life insurance to replace your income. This is a basic rule of thumb that assumes that your family would invest the $500,000 upon your death and hope to get a decent return. To keep the math simple, your family would have to be lucky enough to get a 10% average rate of return on in the stock market to *replace* your income as 10% of $5000,000 is $50,000 each year in earnings that they could use without touching the initial investment. The problem is that this calculation does not account for inflation, increases in income and lifestyle over the years, market volatility, taxes, nor does it accommodate for debt, nor estate taxes.[*]

The hypothetical rates of return shown are assumed on a $500,000 investment. These figures are for illustrative purposes only and do not represent the past or the future performance of any actual investments. These figures do not reflect any fees or charges associated with any investment. If they did, they would be lower then cited above.

Therefore, another great way to calculate the appropriate amount of life insurance is the DIME method.

DIME stands for

Debt

Income

Mortgage

Education

The idea behind this calculation is you add

The cost of **D**ebt (credit card, cars, etc.)

The cost of replacing your **I**ncome (10x your income)

The cost of paying off your **M**ortgage

The cost paying for your kid's college **E**ducation or paying off your student loans.

The issue becomes that most people can't afford the large amount of life insurance if they don't plan appropriately and utilize the proper forms of life insurance.

People in general are procrastinators and the longer they wait to get life insurance the more expensive it is! This is one area that you should never procrastinate. Life insurance is often considered the keystone to a financial plan.

Story of Procrastination

I had a client, a friend of the family actually, that we had gotten the couple underwritten for a $500,000 policy. During the underwriting process they sold their home, paid off some debt, and moved into a newer and nicer home for a total of $600 less than they were paying on their current home and debt payments. The plan was to take the money they were saving monthly with their new lower monthly payments and pay premiums to their life insurance and its subaccount so that they would have not only the life insurance, but a way to accumulate cash value potentially tax free.

They were excited about their plan, and during the underwriting period, they moved into the home. They were underwritten at a perfect rating! I met with them to deliver the policy and they told me that they wanted to "hold off" on the policy! They wanted to use the $600 per month over the next few months to make updates to the new home. They told me that after 6 months their updates should be complete and then they could buy their policy.

I was adamant that their new "plan" was a faulty plan. If they turned down the policy they would have almost no insurance except a tiny policy at work. If a tragedy were to strike, their family would be devastated. If they turned down the policy, they would have to re-test for their rating that determines their cost of insurance in 6 months! What if their health declined?! They may not be able to get this rating and cost again.

They insisted that they had gone this long without life insurance, so "what was another 6 months?" They thanked me for giving them the GIFT of understanding their money. They assured me they would buy the life insurance policy in 6 months and even asked me to set the appointment in my calendar.

I told them again and again… "I advise you not to do this, I advise you not to do this."

Unfortunately, they turned down the policy and just weeks before their follow-up appointment, I got a call from their daughter, my good friend :

She said, "They found a spot on my dad's lung."

The next month she said, "It doubled in size."

Within 8 months he had passed. The family has some updates in their house and some great memories of a great man, but peace of mind knowing that the wife and kids were taken care of was not on their list of blessings.

The moral of the story is that humans by nature think we are invincible and that "it will never happen to me." However, there is one thing that will happen to all of us...one guarantee that everyone in the industry can give to their clients no matter which company, what products they have to offer, etc. The one guarantee is that we all will die. So why not do what you can to prepare for the unavoidable? If the family added the $600/month into the policy for 14 months, for a total of $8,400, upon his death they would have had at least $500,000 to aid their family for years if not generations to come.

Before we move on, let's reiterate and be clear: The main purpose of a life insurance policy is to provide a death benefit. It is not a short-term savings vehicle nor is it ideal for short-term insurance needs. It is designed to be long term in nature and should be purchased only if one has a need for life insurance and the financial ability to keep it in force for a substantial period of time. Surrendering a policy or allowing it to lapse may result in substantial surrender charges and/or tax consequences. Variable Universal Life policies are subject to market risk and should be closely evaluated by someone that is properly licensed. It is called Variable because The Policy Value can vary based on the experience of the investments in the subaccount. Therefore, this type of policy can lose money if the subaccount incurs losses and could put the policy in jeopardy of lapsing. Policy owners should read the prospectus and work closely with their advisor to determine if this would be suitable for their particular situation.

GIFT FIVE

Dollar Cost Averaging

Some people wait until they have a chunk of money saved before they make an investment, while others try to time the market, and yet others just consistently invest the same amount every month no matter what the circumstances. At first glance you would think the last type of person is so nonchalant about their investments that they must be the investor that has the worst results. However, that is generally not the case. The last person is actually practicing a strategy known as **dollar cost averaging.**

Dollar cost averaging is investing the same amount at set intervals. This eliminates the guesswork of trying to time the market.

This is a simple way to see the benefit of dollar-cost averaging:

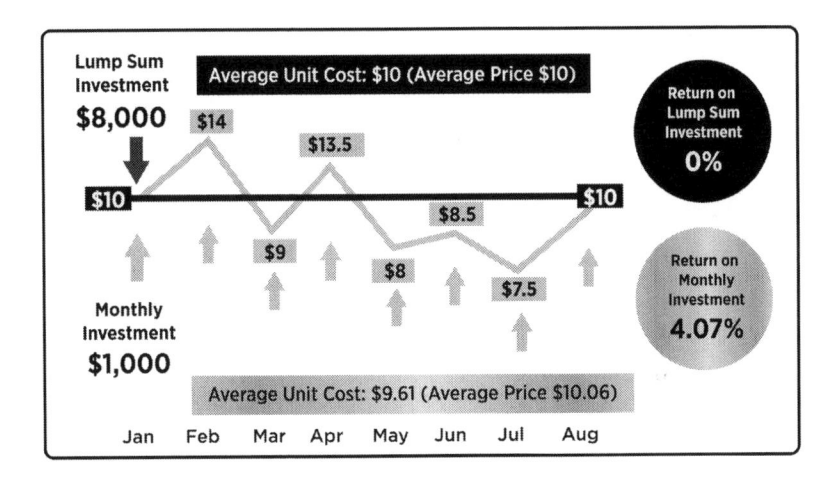

Lump Sum Investment: $8,000
Monthly Investment: $1,000

Prices by month: Jan $10, Feb $14, Mar $13.5, Apr $9, May $8, Jun $8.5, Jul $7.5, Aug $10

Average Unit Cost: $10 (Average Price $10)
Average Unit Cost: $9.61 (Average Price $10.06)

Return on Lump Sum Investment: **0%**
Return on Monthly Investment: **4.07%**

The rates of return chosen are for illustrative purposes only and should not be viewed as an indication of performance for any particular investment. Rate of return is a hypothetical example for illustrative purposes only and does not reflect the actual investment in any product. They do not reflect the performance risks, expenses or charges associated with any actual investment. Different time periods could have different results.

The black straight line shows someone investing $8,000 upfront into an investment. That investment goes up and down in price over 8 months. They initially bought at $10 per share and they decided to sell when the investment was again at $10 per share. That however means that they never made any money. Hence, the 0% rate of return.

However the person that takes an approach of investing that $8,000 by contributing $1,000 per month over the same 8 months would be purchasing at different pricing each month as the market rises and falls. This is seen with the movement of the gray line. So, one month they may buy at $10, the next $14, yet another at $8. In this example the person that invested monthly at different prices came out ahead at 4.07% rate of return although the investment was the same price in month one as it was in the month that they sold.

So in this example the person that practiced **dollar-cost-averaging** experienced a better return on their investment over this time horizon.

Depending on the timing of an investment and the time horizon, it is possible that someone could have better results without dollar cost averaging. If someone was able to foresee that an investment may be at a relatively low price and invests at the "bottom", then they could benefit greatly. Let's refer the chart again. If someone invested the entire $8000 at the lowest price of $7.5 and then sold at $10, they could come out ahead. So, consider if you are savvy and disciplined enough in the investments you are purchasing to know how and when to take advantage of their highs and lows.

In general, dollar cost averaging can help reduce the emotional component of investing while smoothing out the average purchase price of your investment over time. Additionally, for certain investors it can be an affordable and disciplined way to invest by consistently making smaller periodic investments over time.

With that said, dollar cost averaging has its drawbacks. Some would argue that the market tends to rise over time so lump sum investing may actually be better over the long haul since the entire lump sum would have been invested earlier rather than smaller amounts invested at later dates. Additionally, dollar cost averaging is not a substitute for identifying good investment options as poor investments are apt to fall in value regardless of the investment strategy being implemented.

Dollar cost averaging may also result in more fees depending on the account type and often times the strategy just delays systematic risk until later. Dollar cost averaging is generally used in accounts such as 401k's and/or IRAs where consistent, periodic investments can be made and where there are limits to how much can be invested during a calendar year. Consult your financial professional to determine if dollar cost averaging or lump sum investing is right for you and your situation.

Dollar cost averaging features an automated/disciplined strategy, reduces the emotional component, avoids bad timing, and provides convenience. Yet, it is not a substitute for identifying good investments, could cause more fees if you pay per transaction, and could just delay risk.

Investing on a systematic and non-emotional basis is part of an appropriate dollar cost averaging strategy. Investing should not be emotional. Although if you have worked hard for your money it is always hard not to be emotional when it comes to your investments. For many people the money they save is not just numbers on a page. It is their blood, their sweat, their tears; it is their time away from their kids. It's more than emotional; it is *personal.*

So what would work best for you? Would you like to be sure that your investments utilize the concept of dollar-cost-averaging? Can you be disciplined to invest systematically? Or do you prefer investing sporadically when it seems right?

GIFT SIX

TAX EXEMPTIONS

Another area of finance that people tend to be emotional about is their tax refund. Many people like the "feeling" of getting a big tax refund, until they are educated as to what is really happening if they get a large refund.

We see commercials and advertisements, especially during tax season, encouraging us to use XYZ Company so they can get you a larger refund. Sure, sometimes they can help find a deduction that you missed, but never allow them to convince you to decrease your exemptions that you claim with your payroll department so that you will get a larger refund next year!

You see, your refund is money that you are entitled to now! It is called a REFUND because you overpaid your taxes throughout the year. Now, I'm not suggesting that you change your exemptions so that you owe taxes at the end of the year; however, I am suggesting that you work with a tax professional to see what number of exemptions you should claim in order to try to **break even**. You don't want to owe the IRS money, but you don't want them to owe you money either.

If you are due a refund, all that means is the taxes that came out of your check every pay were in excess of what you are obligated to pay!!! So, do you want more money in your pocket by your next pay cycle? Obviously consult your tax advisor first on what you should claim; yet it sometimes is as simple as going to your HR department and just changing the number of exemptions!

What number of exemptions should you claim? Well that's why you need the tax advisor. Any competent CPA or accountant can look at your last set of tax return forms, your situation in the current year, and the tax credits that you are eligible to receive and help you calculate what number of exemptions you should be claiming to *break even*.

Of course, I'm going to encourage you to invest this newly "found" money. Now be aware that you will not have that chunk of money coming to you at the end of the year. But, would you rather hold onto your money throughout the year and have control of how it is utilized or would you like to loan it to the government for a year? If you look at it this way, that "Loan" is interest free, as the government doesn't pay you interest for using your money throughout the year.

For instance, if you have a $4,800 tax refund, work with your tax advisor to allow for that money not to be deducted from your check every pay. There are certain tax credits and such that don't make this calculation as simple as taking that $4,800 and saying that you will now have $400 per month extra in your pocket, but it still may be a significant amount and potentially hundreds of dollars to you each month. This is why a tax advisor is essential in utilizing this concept.

GIFT SEVEN

THE COST OF WAITING

Time can be your worst enemy or your greatest ally. When I saw this example at just 22 years old, I knew I needed to be sure I was saving consistently.

The best way to put time on your side is to start saving TODAY! Here is an example of how the monthly amount required to reach a total savings of $1 million for retirement varies by how much time you have to hit that goal. This illustration shows investing in a hypothetical tax-deferred account and receiving a 8% rate of return annually. If you were trying to reach $1 million of savings at retirement but received a lesser rate of return, you would need to save more.

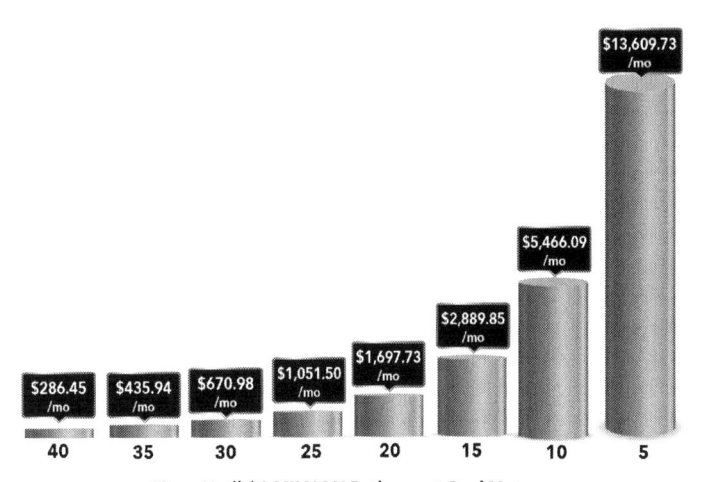

Years Until $1 MILLION Retirement Goal Met

40	35	30	25	20	15	10	5
$286.45/mo	$435.94/mo	$670.98/mo	$1,051.50/mo	$1,697.73/mo	$2,889.85/mo	$5,466.09/mo	$13,609.73/mo

This example shows how the monthly amount required to reach $1 million for retirement changes with how much time you have to hit that goal in an 8% tax-deferred hypothetical account. The best way to put time on your side is to start saving today. In this hypothetical example, an 8% annual compounded rate of return is assumed on hypothetical monthly investments over different time periods. The example is for illustrative purposes only and does not represent any specific investment. It is unlikely that any one rate of return will be sustained over time. This example does not reflect any taxes, or fees and charges associated with any investment. If they had been applied, the period of time to reach a $1 million retirement goal would be longer. Also, keep in mind, that income taxes are due on any gains when withdrawn.

So, the point is to start saving pronto!

Yet, when I have shown this example to many clients that are approaching retirement they seem to find this to be **so** unsettling that they GIVE UP!!! That is not the point of this illustration. The point is that no matter where you are in your life, there is no better time than NOW to start saving. Sure you may not be able to be in a situation to retire *when* you want to, with *how much* you want to, because you waited too long and didn't learn these GIFTs of money; however, the worst thing you can do is throw in the towel. A huge mistake is to assume that you are "too far gone" and then not to utilize these concepts at all! Utilize these concepts even if it is on a smaller scale than you would like.

I tell every client:

<u>Poor</u> **people spend all their money and save what's left over. And what is always left over? Nothing!!!**

<u>Wealthy</u> **people (even before they were wealthy) saved money first and then spent what was left over! That's how they became wealthy.**

So COMMIT! Commit to PAYING YOURSELF FIRST every month and you can build up a nest egg. No matter how big or how small... It is still YOUR NEST EGG!

I was asked just the other day what does it mean when someone says, "Pay yourself first"? This means that every time you receive or earn money, the first thing you do, is you set a portion aside for *you*. This could be in a savings or investment vehicle. At the time of this writing my 9 and 12 year old are well versed at this concept. They know that when they receive a Gift of Money for a birthday or a holiday, they must save HALF of it! Yes HALF. I started this habit as toddlers, as I knew that if they got into the habit of saving half that they would be somewhat on target. Later in life when they have a "real job" it would be reasonable to assume that to reach their goals they will need to allocate at least HALF to taxes and savings…paying themselves first! Although now they sometimes complain that they'd like to keep more of the money for the toy, game, or doll that they desire, I hope that one day they realize that this habit was one of the best Gifts of Money that their mother ever gave them.

Gift Eight

Debt Management

This is a fun category! Fun? Yes it can be very fun to watch the bills that you are receiving in the mail every month just disappear! When you are caught up in the rat race of credit card debt, loans, medical bills, etc. it can be suffocating.

Many people think that if they can just scrape enough to pay a little extra on each bill then they are doing O.K.! No, you are not! STOP! Paying a little extra on all your bills every month WILL pay them down faster than just paying the minimum, but *there is a more efficient way* to eliminate debt.

First off, let's talk about Good Debt versus Bad Debt.

Good debt is when you have leveraged other people's money. Having a mortgage is good debt.[*] Even

---

[*] *There may be pitfalls to owning real estate and there are embedded risks when taking out a mortgage. Good debt is often seen as leverage that has the potential to help you generate income and/or increase your net worth over time. With that said, debt comes with a variety of risk factors that you should consider before borrowing. Here, leverage can be beneficial but can also be detrimental if abused. When purchasing a home for example, be sure you can afford the payments, now and into the future.*

billionaires finance some of their properties or businesses. People often wonder why a billionaire would finance something if they have the cash to pay for it. LEVERAGE. Now, in this book we will stick to the basics as an entire book can be dedicated to this topic alone and they have. We will just scratch the surface so you have a starting point.

Let's be Clear: There is no "One Size Fits All" strategy. The below strategies are not appropriate for everyone and consider all options before making a decision. Sometimes what's best is not what makes us comfortable. Sometimes what's best is not what is most familiar to us either. Individual circumstances are a key factor in determining a course of action. Consider if these Debt Basics may be appropriate for the situation at hand.

Debt Basic #1: For most people having a mortgage on their home would be smart. This is how you leverage other people's money... The bank's money. If you get a loan from the bank at 5% interest, and you get to write off that interest on your taxes; that fits into the definition of GOOD DEBT! When practicing this methodology, individuals don't worry about how long it takes to pay it off or if they have a mortgage on their home upon their death. Remember consult a properly licensed individual about how and if your situation qualifies you for these benefits.

If you have the cash, should you pay for a home in cash? Not usually!

Why not?

    A. You won't get the tax write off

    B. You won't get the cash invested and gaining interest

For example: If you took out a $100,000 loan at 5% interest and you still had $100,000 invested in the market gaining anything above an average 5%, then you win!!

Most people in America today don't have the cash to buy a house out right so they just take the loan and then pay EXTRA every month or pay bi-weekly to try to get the mortgage paid off sooner.

People seem to think that once they have their house paid off then they can start saving more money monthly. First of all, most people won't stay in the same house for 10-30 years. Also, remember The Cost Of Waiting? If you wait 15-30 years to START saving, then it will take a lot more cash per month to save a decent amount for retirement. Sure if the house is paid off they would have equity in the home, but it is literally stuck in the house and they won't be able to access it as they would a liquid investment.

Reasons to Pay off your Mortgage Sooner

1. To have more money monthly at a later date to save for retirement.
2. You may "feel" more secure that you own your residence.
3. You will no longer be required to pay interest.
4. Things to Consider:
   - Most people will never save the entire amount they were once paying toward the mortgage!
   - The Cost of Waiting: You will have to save a lot more to reach your goal if you start later!
   - You will no longer pay interest and therefore no longer have the tax write off.

Reasons to Keep a Mortgage for 30 Years or Longer

1. Leverage! Borrow the banks money under 5% and then allow your money to grow at a larger percentage
2. The Tax Deduction
3. Money is a GIFT!!! Having money/cash on hand is essential. Don't tie up all your money/cash in the equity of your home.
4. Things to Consider: You may not always be able to leverage and get a larger rate of return on your money than the interest that you are paying on a mortgage. Work with a properly licensed investment professional and tax professional to be sure the tax write off and the potential

investment gains are congruent with your risk tolerance, current portfolio, and particular situation. Not everyone should hold debt and tax deductions could be seen as the government subsidizing your mortgage. Since tax laws have the ability to change, be sure to consult a tax professional for the option that is right for you.

There is no better GIFT than the GIFT of CASH!

Many people think that if they need the cash in their home that they can access it. There are a lot of people that have a check book that is attached to a home equity loan from their bank and they believe that if they get in a pinch that they can just write a check. Well, think again. We saw in 2009 that banks revoked home equity lines. People who once thought they had an "emergency fund" with their home equity loan or were paying extra payments on their mortgage so when little Suzie went to college they could just write a check from the line of credit, found themselves in a pickle!

Be wise! Not everyone should "buy" a home. There are risks in leveraging your home. You must be able to pay your payments on time, be sure to have an emergency fund, and have a backup plan. If you buy a home in one town and your employment suddenly requires you to move, would you be able to rent out the property or would it be marketable to sell quickly?

There are many factors to consider before you mortgage a property.

Debt Basic #2: Your student loans may have provisions for lower payments and even have a provision to waive a portion of the balance. It is time consuming, but worth the effort to check with the Department of Education and see what programs you are eligible. There are many companies that will charge a fee to help you through this process. Beware of any company that will charge a fee and says that in the end they will repair your credit. That means they *will* damage your credit first! Go through an attorney, if it is too cumbersome for you to do yourself.

Look at it like doing your taxes. You can try to do it yourself or you can hire a professional to handle it for you. I know it sounds expensive to hire an attorney, but that isn't always the case. We have found some great firms that can assist our clients for way less than some of these so-called "Student Loan Resource Centers" that charge an arm and a leg and damage your credit.

Debt Basic #3: You may NOT need to declare bankruptcy! Especially beware if you are ineligible for Chapter 7 Bankruptcy, which wipes away your debt, and you are thinking of claiming Chapter 13 bankruptcy.

- Chapter 13 Bankruptcy is a restructuring of debt and you still have to pay off all the debt!
- Both Chapter 13 and Chapter 7 damage your credit and may prohibit certain employment.

There are debt roll down programs that work just as well and in certain situations can still get the debt paid off, yet not damage your credit. I offer clients a calculation and debt pay down plan for free so they can get in a better situation so they can one day invest more in their future.

Debt Basic #4: Don't pay extra on EACH debt. A more efficient way to pay off debt is to pay the card or debt with the **highest cost index first**. The cost index is the minimum payment divided by the balance.

The illustration I created below should help illustrate a typical debt situation. Most people would round up from the minimum payment and just pay extra on EACH debt. In this illustration, the client is paying $1455 total each month; yet, the minimum payments are only $1179. So that's an extra $276 per month, but they spread the $276 over 9 debts! That is not the most efficient way to pay off their debt. Rather they could calculate the cost index on each debt and pay the debt with the highest cost index first.

DEBT ROLL-DOWN CALCULATOR

CREDIT CARD	APR	BALANCE	MINIMUM PAYMENT	ACTUAL PAYMENT	COST INDEX
Sams	18.00%	$180.00	$35.00	$55.00	0.1944
Car Loan	3.00%	$2,303.00	$350.00	$350.00	0.1520
Macys	24.50%	$574.00	$75.00	$100.00	0.1307
Sears	19.90%	$548.00	$50.00	$100.00	0.0912
JC Penny	28.00%	$947.00	$65.00	$100.00	0.0686
Capital One	18.00%	$2,983.00	$204.00	$250.00	0.0684
Chase	22.00%	$3,382.00	$220.00	$250.00	0.0651
Home Depot	18.90%	$2,702.00	$150.00	$200.00	0.0555
Walmart	18.00%	$686.00	$30.00	$50.00	0.0437
			$1,179.00	$1,455.00	

They should pay the minimum on all the debts except the debt with the highest cost index. In this example it is the Sam's Club Card. They should take the $276 and add that to the $35 minimum payment that they were paying on the Sam's Club Card until it is paid off. They will have the Sam's Club Card paid off in the first month! Once it is paid off, they should then pay the extra to the debt with the **next** highest cost index, which would be the car loan.

So,

$35/month that was paid to Sam's Club that's now paid off

+$276/month extra that was used to spread over all the debts

+$350/month that was being paid on the car loan

$661/month is the total per month that should be applied to the car loan until it is paid off **and then** they should work their way down the line of debts.

Follow along with the example below and you can see how, if followed, this method will accelerate debt pay-down. The risk is if someone is not disciplined enough to use the extra money to pay down one debt at a time, as then this would not work out well. Obviously they must also continue to pay the minimum on each debt to maintain a good credit situation.

$276.00	Total Monthly Payments less Minimum Payments	
+$35.00	Sam's Minimum Payment	
$311.00	New Monthly Sams Payment	

Sam's Balance	Monthly Payment	Months to Pay Off
$180.00	$311.00	0.6

Car Loan Payment Plan

$311.00 Previous payment to Sam's
+ $350.00 Car Loan Minimun Payment
$661.00 New Monthly Car Loan Payment

Car Loan Balance	Monthly Payment	Months to Pay Off
$2,303.00	$661.00	3.5

Macy's Payment Plan

$661.00 Previous payment to Car Loan
+ $75.00 Macy's Minimun Payment
$736.00 New Monthly Macy's Payment

Macy's Balance	Monthly Payment	Months to Pay Off
$574.00	$736.00	0.8

Sears Payment Plan

$736.00 Previous payment to Macys
+ $50.00 Sears Minimun Payment
$786.00 New Monthly Sears Payment

Sears Balance	Monthly Payment	Months to Pay Off
$548.00	$786.00	0.7

JC Penny Payment Plan

$786.00 Previous payment to Sears
+ $65.00 JC Penny Minimun Payment
$851.00 New Monthly JC Penny Payment

JC Penny Balance	Monthly Payment	Months to Pay Off
$947.00	$851.00	1.1

In this example, the client would have their debt paid off years faster by applying this simple concept!

There are debt roll-down calculators available online that will illustrate roll-down by interest rate, balance, etc. Structuring your debt repayment on cost -index can be an efficient method of debt pay down. Consider other methods of repaying debt to determine which method may be right for you.

GIFT NINE
MORTGAGES

In this chapter we will get into a bit more detail on the a few different mortgage options. The first thing to know about a mortgage is buying a house you can comfortably afford in which you can still save enough to meet your retirement goals can be advantageous for most people. Only buying a home once you have a significant emergency built up to help when there are unexpected expenses can also be advantageous for most people.

There are many mortgage options to choose from when buying or re-financing a home. Everyone's personal situations are different. In the long-run most people will benefit from having an option that gives them the smallest payment OBLIGATION. Even when someone decides to pay extra on a mortgage, financing the home with the *option* that gives the lowest payment OBLIGATION may come in handy. This way, if something tragic should happen, there would be the *option* to pay the lower payment.

When I saw side-by-side examples of the impact that various mortgage scenarios have on the overall impact of a family's financial picture, I realized right away that people needed educated on what the different mortgage options are and which is best for their long-term situation. Not every situation is the same and there is not a One-Size-Fits-All solution; however, I started to question if it made sense to pay extra on a mortgage or invest the extra. I also started to question if it may be best for some people to continue to have a mortgage to maintain a tax write off.

Many people buy a home and never compare the long-term effects on their overall financial picture. In the chart below we see a choice between a 30 year "Traditional" mortgage, a 15 year "Traditional" mortgage, and an "Alternative" Interest Only loan. The term "Traditional" refers to a mortgage where you pay interest and principal. The "Alternative" Interest Only Loan refers to exactly what it is called… Interest ONLY. The "Alternative" Interest Only Loan could be a Home Equity Line of Credit or even an ARM/Adjustable Rate Mortgage.

Some people panic when they see Interest Only and think "Oh my! Then I'll never pay off my Mortgage?" That's not what I mean. You can indeed continue to refinance with Interest Only loans forever and *leverage* your money. However, this is only wise if you are investing the money that you save by using this lower payment option when financing your home.

Yet, I am not an advocate of investing the difference in non-liquid, non-accessible investments like more real estate and not diversifying your portfolio. We saw many successful individuals do this prior to 2008 and when the real estate market tanked they had no cash to get them through the crisis. Even worse was that many people saw the value of their home sink below what they owed on their mortgage. Picking a mortgage option that would allow them to set some cash aside to help them through the crisis could have been beneficial.

Before we go into some examples, I want to clarify that these are hypothetical examples and they are for illustrative purposes only. Mortgage option and investment strategies vary based on the needs and wants of the customer. Illustrated investment returns are based upon annual average interest rates. It is unlikely that any one rate of return will be sustained over time. Lower average rates of returns would illustrate different potentially less advantageous results. If someone has a consistent negative average rate of return over a long period of time, then these scenarios would obviously need to reflect their returns. Each scenario should take into account risk tolerance as well as the long-term intention for the property.

The example is for illustrative purposes only and does not represent any specific investment.

Also it is important to understand that interest rate and your ability to qualify for certain mortgage options can vary based on a number of factors. Generally lenders will base their decisions on your credit score, earnings, debt-to-income, down payment amount, cash reserves, mortgage insurance, price of home, closing costs, and intent of use (i.e. investment property versus primary residence). Therefore, depending on these factors and the type of loan, the amount you are able to borrow can vary greatly as can the interest rate.

Many people will choose a mortgage based on the interest rate. Just because a mortgage option has a lower interest rate, does not mean that it will be the most beneficial for the overall financial picture. Different types of loans have different rates. The illustration we are about to discuss shows the typical variation in interest rates for the various product types discussed if all other factors remained the same.

So, let's dig into this chart to get an idea of the different financing methods. If you are buying an average home for $200,000 and went with the "Traditional" method, you would traditionally put 20% down which would be $40,000. On a 15 year note your monthly payment would be $1224 at 4.5% and on a 30 year $859 at 5%.

	Traditional 15 Year	Traditional 30 Year	Alternative Interest Only
Interest Rate	4.5%	5%	5.25%
Home Price	$200,000	$200,000	$200,000
Down Payment	$40,000	$40,000	$20,000
Monthly Payment	$1,224	$859	$788
Upfront Investment	$0	$0	$20,000
Monthly Investment Year 1-15	$0	$365	$436
ROR on Investments	8%	8%	8%
Investments After 15 Years	$0	$118,926	$205,503
Monthly Investment Years 15-30	$1,224	$365	$436
Investment After 30 Years	$398,810	$496,180	$793,950

In this hypothetical example, an 8% annual compounded rate of return is assumed on hypothetical monthly investments over different time periods. The example is for illustrative purposes only and does not represent any specific investment. It is unlikely that any one rate of return will be sustained over time. This example does not reflect any taxes, or fees and charges associated with any investment. If they had been applied, the hypothetical returns would be lower. Also, keep in mind, that income taxes are due on any gains when withdrawn.

If you took the "Alternative" method and financed your home with an interest only mortgage and

- only contributed $20,000 of your $40,000 of cash towards a down payment,
- invested the remaining $20,000,

- as well as invested the difference between your low $788/month "Interest" Only payment and the $1224/month "Traditional" Payment,

then you would find yourself in an interesting position.

You see in both the traditional methods you have no upfront money invested. So with the 15 Year "Traditional" Mortgage you would pay off your house in 15 years and Traditionally you would invest the $1224/month that you used to pay in mortgage payments for the NEXT 15 years. That being the case and if the investments grew at an 8% rate of return, you would have a paid off house and would have $398,810 at the end of 30 years.

This method has some risks. In all my years with clients I rarely see someone pay off their mortgage and actually save what they used to pay in mortgage payments. Life Happens! Something usually comes up that takes the place of this expense. Besides the fact that most people rarely stay in their home that long, as people age they suffer illnesses, job losses, family crises, etc. that usually eat up that money that they used to pay towards the mortgage. Maybe it's human nature, maybe it's lack of discipline, maybe it's just getting older; but, that is the trend. Needless to say, I have had met countless clients that come to me when they find themselves in a bind when they have had a job loss and have no cash to help them pay their payments. Also, when you are jobless you can't qualify for a home equity loan to access the cash that is literally stored in the walls of your home in the form of "equity". Therefore, the 15 Year Traditional Mortgage may be right for some people, but may not be right for everyone.

Let's take a look what would happen if you chose the 30 year mortgage instead of the 15 year. In this example you save the $365/month difference between the 30 year and the 15 year payments. After 15 years, you will still owe $108,614. This examples show that you would have enough to pay it off if you saved the $365/month difference and assumed an 8% rate of return on your money. So, if you lose your job or become ill, you have some choices. You could use the $118,926 to help pay your mere $859/month payments, OR you could pay off the house and still have over $10,000, OR you could just keep letting that $118,926 compound and pay the mortgage payment! If you allowed the money to compound and continued to add the $365/month for the remainder of the 30 year loan, you would have $496,108 in investments assuming an 8% rate of return. Also, at this point the house is paid off! Therefore, the 30 Year Traditional Mortgage may be right for some people, but may not be right for everyone.

Now look at the "Alternative" Interest Only option. Although this option may not be right for everyone, if you started with the $20,000 you saved from not making a big down payment, added the $436/month difference between the interest only payment and the 30 year payment, and got an 8% rate of return, you would have $205,503 in cash at year 15. Yes you still owe $180,000 on your mortgage but you have the cash **on hand** to pay it off whenever you would like. This idea of having the money on hand to pay off the mortgage maybe attractive to some people while others can't grasp the benefit of leveraging their money.

If you decided to pay the house off in year 15 with the cash you have accumulated, you would have $10,312 left in cash with the 30 year option and $25,503 left in cash with the Interest Only option. Obviously if you chose the 15 year option, at the end of 15 years, the house would be paid off, but you would have $0 accumulated.

What if you continued through the 30 years paying the Interest Only and investing the difference? Well, if you continued to invest the $436/month difference, by the time the 30 years rolled around, you would have almost $793,950 SAVED!!!! This would allow for the $180,000 mortgage to be paid off and still have a nice sum saved for retirement.

Although you will often see that people who understand how money works often choose to carry a big, long mortgage and never pay it off, I want to be crystal clear. None of the listed mortgage examples are right for everyone and each personal situation is different.

Choosing a mortgage based on interest rate only may not be the best decision. With all other factors being equal, typically a 15 year mortgage may have a slightly lower rate offer than the 30 year and interestingly the interest only could also be lower than the traditional 30 year with promotional rates, which typically end after a set time period. Yet, in this example we illustrated the Interest Only option assuming the highest rate. As you can see, the overall picture should be evaluated and not just the interest rate. Even though the **interest rate is higher**, the **payment is slightly lower**. So evaluating the overall picture and how it will effect the overall situation is key!

Also, since the example is based on an average 8% rate of return we must discuss what happens if the market is down. Well, first of all, the average 8% rate of return was used to take into consideration that some years there will be a higher gain than 8% and some years the account may lose. That's why the illustration shows and **average** of 8% rate of return. There is the chance of the account being down in a year that the money is needed, and that is a risk…**A huge risk that must be considered carefully.**

This is similar to the risk of the value of the real estate as well. If you must sell the house in a particular year, the house may not have the value that it would in another year. Any investment has risk and these risks should be considered. Getting married, runs you the risk of getting divorced, as you cannot get divorced if you were never married. Getting in a car, runs you the risk of getting in an accident. As with anything, weigh if the risk is outweighed by the reward for you and your situation. If you want to buy a home, look at the different options, evaluate the risks for your situation and be sure you are in a financially secure position with a sufficient emergency fund, down payment, and that you can comfortably afford the mortgage payment and still save and invest for your future.

You may want to look at it this way. If you try to pay down or pay off the mortgage it is the same as "saving" your money in an investment that:

- **Is not liquid.** - You can't access your "savings"/equity unless the absolute right person comes along to buy the property so you can get your cash out. Maybe you could qualify for another loan to get cash out, but that's not necessarily quick nor liquid.
- **Is subject to volatility.** - The housing market determines the value of your investment and is as fickle as a weather issue, or a large local employers going out of business, or other neighbors foreclosing. All of which leave your investment subject to volatility.
- **Is not diversified.**- You have all your eggs in one basket.
- **Is not allowing you to dollar cost average.**- You are actually paying down very little in the beginning in principal on a typical mortgage.
- **Is not giving you tax benefits.** - Paying off the mortgage sooner actually eliminates tax benefits.

Again, the mortgage option that has the lowest payment OBLIGATION will leave you with more cash in hand. The worse case scenario, you can pay extra when you *want* to; but, can pay the minimum OBLIGATION if you *need* to. Imagine if you use the GIFTS of Money that you now know to grow an investment account to become equivalent to or even more than the mortgage balance! You would have this money available to you in an account that at any time you could withdraw the funds and "pay off" your mortgage. There is more peace of mind knowing that you have the ability to pay off your mortgage, but that you are being smart with your GIFT of Money. This is making your money work harder for you so you don't have to work so hard for your money!

So remember, There is no "One Sized Fits All" recommendation for what mortgage will work best every time; yet there are some key elements to guide you:

- Pick a mortgage that is affordable now and into the future.
- Invest any money you save by choosing a mortgage with the lower payment OBLIGATION.
- A Longer mortgage option usually Lowers the monthly payment OBLIGATION.

- An Interest Only option typically Lowers the payment OBLIGATION.

- Maintaining a mortgage may allow you to maintain the tax write off of the mortgage interest.

GIFT TEN
PLANNING

Being a young female in the industry I had a lot of obstacles when I first started. I was *told* that being a female in the industry would give me challenges galore. On the contrary, it has been a Gift, as my clients have a tendency to be more honest with me and trust me more than they do my male counterparts. As I took on this career, I was asked by some naysayers in my family, "Who wants to listen to a 22 year old about their money?"

I was discouraged at first then decided to change my paradigm and look at my age as a Gift when someone asked me an interesting question. They asked, "If your computer broke and you wanted to have it fixed, would you go to your 17 year old neighbor and ask for help or the 70 year old neighbor?" The obvious answer is the 17 year old!! I realized right then that the same applies to money! I'd rather take advice from the successful young financial professional, than the broke, old, advisor that still has to work at age 70. Older doesn't equal wiser.

That question changed my mind forever about how I viewed my career and how I knew I could help people regardless of their age, gender, or background. I knew at that moment that if I knew more than the man that was 20-30 years my senior, that I would be the one with more *value* for clients.

I had such a passion to share these concepts and help people, that I went on a mission to gain the knowledge to become *valuable* to my clients. I got the licenses, the training, the mentors and the experience. It became apparent that *knowledge was power* and if I knew more than any of my older, more tenured counterparts, my age, nor my gender, nor my location, nor my ethnicity mattered. More important than my own knowledge was to know who had even more knowledge and leverage their knowledge. I became an expert in finding experts! I developed a network of mentors and experts that I could call upon in areas that were not my forte.

When it comes to planning, I always say, **people don't plan to fail they simply fail to plan.** Planning is important but having a **GREAT** planner is even more important. If you want **good** results go to someone that is **good** at what they do. If you want **great** results go to someone that is **great** at what they do.

Remember time and experience doesn't necessarily make someone **great**. Just because someone has been in the industry forever or is your dad's golfing buddy, does not mean they have **great** advice. By all means, also don't take advice from the guy working on the line next to you that has the same crappy job as you but has some money saved! And, absolutely don't try to perform "money surgery" yourself. If you had to have a medical surgery, would you research it on the internet and see how to perform the surgery and then **try to do it yourself**?! No! You would go to the best surgeon and have them perform the surgery. They have the skills to do the job the best! Don't pretend that you are the most skilled "surgeon" when it comes to investing! Find a skilled and properly licensed financial professional and let them do the best surgery on your finances as possible.

One of my mentors always says: "Know what you don't know, know who knows what you don't know and that's all you need to know."

Therefore, in my opinion, the best way to identify the best "surgeon" for your money, is that they know what subjects in which they are NOT the best, in which subjects they ARE, and they know how to FIND and utilize others that are the best. For example, I don't try to day trade my client's accounts; I use an active money manger. I don't try to give tax advice; I work with a CPA. I don't try to do a surgery myself when someone is more qualified; I bring in the best TEAM of "surgeons" to operate on their specialty of my client's finances.

Also, when choosing an advisor, find someone who isn't in it for the money. Hard to do, as this is what they do for a living, right? What I mean is, don't go to someone that charges you an arm and a leg to put together the plan or that has a minimum account size. You may meet the minimum and feel "special" that you **qualify** to get the "high end guy" in town. But, that's BS. He's only concentrating on high-end clients because he *is* in it for the money.

When it comes to planning be sure you don't have just **A** goal in mind, but **many** goals. Make sure your advisor looks at 4 categories of your finances before making any suggestions:

How much you make,

How much you spend,

How much you have, and

How much you owe.

Without those 4 basics, they can't make an educated suggestion. I always say "garbage in, garbage out". If you give me garbage (or partial) information, you can only expect to get garbage advice (not necessarily correct advice for your overall situation).

Talk about your money. I don't mean to not be private. Money is private and the entire world does not need to know what you have. What I mean is that you should talk about your money with your advisor and with your family. Many clients will hide information from their advisor. Sometimes it is because they are embarrassed that they have debt or that they don't make as much as they think they "should." I view it like the patient that has diabetes and doesn't want to tell the doctor that they sneak some dessert every night after their spouse goes to bed. This type of behavior can be dangerous to your financial health… Clue in your advisor!

The same goes for your family. It is the right thing to let your family know about the diseases and medical complications that you have so that they know what to watch for in their own health. If you have a family history of cancer, they should know about it. The same goes for your financial health. If you have money complications, they should learn from it. If you are financially healthy, they should learn from it. Another Gift of Money is for people to learn from the mistakes and successes of others. Talk to your kids, your family, and your friends about money, protecting it, insurance, and what you are doing with your money. The only way to benefit the next generation is to talk about it.

Bring your kids to see your advisor. Let them experience how to make and save money. If they see how you struggle with debt, they may simply repeat that behavior. But, if they witness how you search for a cure and overcome it, they too will overcome it. They may even take the steps to prevent financial health complications in their own lives.

So, I hope you get the point! Pass this book on, schedule an appointment with and advisor today, and send your friends and family to do the same. The only way to cure the financial disease is to give people a GIFT...a GIFT of knowledge ...give the Gift of Money.

Made in the USA
Columbia, SC
17 June 2025